STANDBY

*A Guide for Aspiring Journalists and
Early Career Broadcast Journalists*

Anna-Lysa Gayle

ISBN: 979-8-218-00610-5

Library of Congress Control Number: 2022909168

Printed in the United States of America

CONTENTS

ABOUT THE AUTHOR

Anna-Lysa Gayle served as a nightside reporter and anchor in the nation's capital for nearly six years, where she shared more than two thousand stories and earned multiple awards, including five Emmy awards. This book offers genuine advice for aspiring journalists and early career broadcast professionals.

INTRODUCTION

With sweat trickling down my body on a hot summer's day, and my nerves shooting through the roof, I conquered my first TV news live shot in May 2013. My biggest fear didn't play out. The lines I had written down didn't magically disappear from my mind like I thought they would. I didn't repeatedly stutter as I had envisioned multiple times. I looked a little nervous and perhaps I didn't seem as confident as I do now. The topic didn't thrill me. It wasn't the hard-hitting journalism I fantasized about in journalism school. The topic was "how to choose the right sunscreen," a fun, lighthearted way to begin my career.

I'm writing this book as a letter to my younger self. When I started at Howard University at seventeen years old, there was so much I wanted to know before entering the classroom.

I had so many questions about what my life would be like in four to five years. Now that I've worked professionally in the broadcast journalism field for nearly a decade, I feel comfortable sharing some of my journey with you. It was a tough decision. As usual, fear tries to creep up, causing you to wonder if you're oversharing or breaking some of the unwritten rules.

My journey in journalism hasn't been easy, but there have been lots of great moments. Although, depending on who you ask—looking from the outside in, you may believe something different. There have been lots of tears and self-doubt. This is my chance to reflect on the moments that worked and the moments that didn't, while answering your questions. There's the saying: "If it was easy, everyone would do it." I believe that applies to journalism now more than ever.

It's important to me that this book is filled with the information I was searching for while pursuing a career as a TV news reporter, while trying to figure out how to navigate an industry that can seem very intimidating. While I would love to have tons of mentees, it's impossible for me to reach dozens of people at the same time. This book is my way of answering the many questions I've received about navigating the news industry at a young age.

I didn't grow up with lots of money, but I was raised

with lots of love and the understanding that I could achieve any and all goals, through prayer and hard work. During my senior year, I worked two jobs to make ends meet, while I accepted an unpaid internship for experience. Thankfully, it paid off and it can pay off for you, too. However, I will add that I've also accepted several paid internships, through great organizations that I will discuss later.

My Story

I got my start in journalism in 2013, a week before my graduation. I was an eager twenty-one-year-old with nothing to lose and lots to gain. I was fresh out of journalism school with a lot to prove to myself and so much to learn. Was I scared? Yes, absolutely. However, my goal was to get a job after graduation and not just any job, a job in my field. It was an accomplishment that I had dreamed and cried about many times.

In my first job at WHSV-TV, I made $10.00 per hour starting out. It was less than I was making as a senior with a full-time job on-campus, and a part-time job on weekends. It was a risky financial decision for sure. As a Jamaican immigrant, I was always encouraged to pursue jobs in the medical field, but I somehow found myself attracted to the high-speed world of journalism. The thought of covering a new story every day was exciting. I couldn't wait to explore local news as a general assignment reporter, like the others I'd watched growing up.

I didn't have an agent in my first two jobs. I secured those positions through networking and social media, believe it or not. If there's anything I'd like you to walk away with from this book, it's that you don't need to have rich and famous parents to be a journalist. You just need to have passion, creativity, and integrity and everything else will fall into place. Feel free to contact me with questions you'd like answered. As I continue to grow, so will this book. Enjoy!

CHAPTER 1

Things to Consider Before Becoming a
Broadcast Journalist

In my opinion, the best journalists are those who genuinely care about people and the topics they are covering. So, how do you prepare for a job in broadcast journalism? For me, the answer is simple. First, prepare your heart and your mind, and everything else will fall into place. Before I applied to Howard University, I narrowed down a list of careers that interested me. My mom, who was a police officer in Jamaica, always taught me to give back. I've always wanted to carry on her legacy as a public servant, but I wasn't brave enough to be a police officer. I didn't like the thought of carrying around a gun or arresting people. So, I thought about other options that would give me the same euphoria I'd feel without the duties I was uncomfortable doing. I somehow ended up with journalism, as I narrowed down my list.

As a child, I had a tape recorder that I would record my voice on and play it back to myself. I also had a diary that I filled with my secrets and much more. I even continued writing in my diary as I got older. Journalism was an obvious choice for me. It was something I was already subconsciously doing. I knew it would come as second nature to me. If you're still trying to figure it out, it's okay. There's time.

Questions to Ask Yourself Before Considering Broadcast Journalism

- **Do you like talking to people and learning about their stories?**

When I first told my dad that I was interested in journalism, one of the first questions he asked was "Are you a people person?" At the time, I just nodded and said, "Yes, of course." My first job was at Dunkin' Donuts and it taught me a lot about customer service, but journalism is another beast. TV news requires serving hundreds of thousands of customers (also known as viewers). Instead of serving one client, I'm now serving different demographics (men, women, sports lovers, fashion lovers, community activists, and more).

There are times you'll be required to knock on strangers' doors, not knowing what's on the other side. Social skills are extremely important for landing interviews, but it could also be key to finding stories. If people feel connected to you, they are more likely to share their secrets with you.

- **Do you like working under pressure?**

Not going to lie, there's a lot of pressure in this business. Pressure from viewers, pressure from your managers and producers, and sometimes it feels like you're carrying the weight of the world. Every single word that comes out of your mouth matters, and every single word carries weight. So, check your script over and over again, until you're comfortable. Oh, and yes, there's this little thing called a deadline that creeps up on you every now and again. "Making slot," as it's called, is very important in this business. As a reporter, you can throw off a whole show by missing your time slot. Viewers are depending on you and are sometimes promised information ahead of time that you must deliver on.

You'll also want to "make slot" to keep your producers happy, because if you fail, so does their show. Sucks, I know. Stress management is a major part of getting through the day-to-day in the journalism industry. There can be many things that trigger stress in your workday. From juggling multiple conversations with sources, to dealing with proper time management.

- **How would you react to uncomfortable situations? Are you willing to talk to people with different views?**

I've interviewed a mother who dressed her son as a member of the Ku Klux Klan, and I've interviewed a teacher who believed in white supremacy. In both instances, I tried to share their story as fairly as I could—given the circumstances.

If you're not good at holding your tongue, you should probably think about another career path that will allow you to be more vocal. Journalism requires you to remove yourself from the equation to shed light on the subject matter at hand. The key is to allow viewers to form their own opinions, without intertwining your own opinions.

- **Are you willing to move around the country?**

Being homesick is a serious side effect at times in this business, especially if you're a family-oriented person. I didn't realize how difficult it would be for me to be hundreds of miles away from my family, until I had to do it for work. Add holidays to the mix and some days I feel selfish for making this choice. Having understanding family members will make the ordeal a little easier.

Since 2013, when I got my start, I've lived in six apartments in four states. I've moved most of my life, so it was nothing new for me, but that doesn't have to be your life. If you find a position in a market that you love, I highly recommend that you settle down. At the end of the day, being comfortable and surrounded by love is what matters most.

- **Are you willing to work odd shifts?**

There are some days that will require working long shifts (e.g., hurricane coverage, protests, mass shootings, other breaking news). Sometimes, you'll make the decision to volunteer, and at other times it will be mandatory. If you're a parent, it can be tough to maneuver. It's best to always prepare a babysitter as a backup.

Sometimes, news will break late in your shift and you'll have to stay late to make sure viewers get the most up-to-date information. If you're not willing to be flexible with your shift, it will likely hurt your career.

- **Are you willing to remove your personal beliefs?**

I've had so many strong opinions that I've kept to myself or saved in drafts on Twitter. Nothing is worth sharing that could lead to an unproductive debate, especially on Twitter (a very public forum). I have a journal where I write out my most controversial thoughts. I'm committed to finding my voice and honing my craft, but not necessarily sharing my opinions. There is a difference between a reporter and a political analyst.

People will ask for your opinions and it's wise to decline the invitation to spill the beans. On the other hand, if you sign up to be a political analyst, you're paid to share your opinions on TV. Those are the panelists that you usually see anchors interviewing on networks like CNN and MSNBC.

- **Are you willing to work overtime with no pay (starting out)?**

  If I collected money for every single project I did outside of work, I would be rich. I've stayed late without pay. I've worked on stories before my shift started. I've written stories on my day off. Those aren't complaints. Those are the facts when you're passionate about the stories you tell. When I get excited about the stories I'm writing, it's hard to walk away, even when I'm technically off the clock. My philosophy has always been to keep producing quality content and the money will come.

- **Are you willing to work odd hours?**

  The typical shifts in local TV news are 3:00 a.m. to noon, 9:30 a.m. to 6:00 p.m., and 3:00 p.m. to 11:30 p.m. All those shifts can go overtime, depending on the day (if there's breaking news or additional projects you're working on).

- **How will you respond to negative comments from viewers?**

I can show you story after story, where news personalities were sent mean comments about their appearances and more. I learned this lesson quite a few times when I first started. I would go to Facebook after my story aired and read the comments and then I realized that people generally don't have nice things to say when they are sitting behind their computers, with lots of time on their hands. I hardly read the comments about my stories, on Facebook, especially, for that very reason. People can be cruel when discussing a subject matter about which they are passionate. Occasionally, viewers may send rude messages. It's your responsibility to choose your battles wisely. I rarely respond to negative comments, but when I do, my responses are well thought out.

Many news organizations have social media policies about how and when you can respond to viewers' comments. In some instances, your response could become a story for entertainment sites. Always keep in mind that you're under a microscope, and my general rule is: you never want to be the story. When you become the story, it can distract from your work. If you're someone who has a hard time controlling your responses, start working on that before you get into the business.

- **Do you mind being a local celebrity?**

This is something I've always struggled with because I love being a journalist, but I never really considered the celebrity aspect. Being a local celebrity can be tough when it comes to privacy. As a public figure, privacy technically goes out the window. Everything you share online is free game. Just something to consider.

CHAPTER 2

Landing Your First Internship

I get this question all the time. There are so many great internships and fellowships out there for high school and college students. In this chapter, I'll list a few organizations and sites you should check out to get more plugged in with opportunities available.

I will start by saying, in order to secure one of these internships, you must first work on your writing skills, punctuality, and attention to detail. Most internships in the journalism industry are unpaid, but they should all be treated like a potential job interview every day while you're completing the internship. You never know when an opportunity may be available at a news station, or other company with whom you are working. This applies to every industry.

Internships are available at almost every local and national news organization in the country. Companies need good interns just as much as interns need them. A good intern, who may recognize areas that need improvement over time or expose gaps that need to be filled immediately, can be a great asset to a company.

Start by identifying the local news station or news outlet you'd like to work for, and on their website, click on the "careers" tab. You'll likely notice a section for students and internships. Click the apply button and follow through with the application process and give it a few weeks. If you don't get a response, you can check in with the internship coordinator at the organization (I would only do this once in a polite e-mail).

Another option is to use sites like Indeed.com, LinkedIn. com, TVJobs.com, and JournalismJobs.com. I also highly recommend signing up with advocacy organizations like the National Association of Black Journalists (NABJ), National Association of Hispanic Journalists (NAHJ), Society of Professional Journalists (SPJ), National Association of Broadcasters (NAB), The Online News Association (ONA), and Investigative Reporters & Editors (IRE). I'm sure there are more out there, but those are some of the most popular ones.

Quickly browse through each organization's website and look at the opportunities available for students. They each have a conference every year, where students can get even more acclimated to their organization. Those conferences are also good places to find mentors who can help you formulate a plan for success.

Another option is to attend journalism career fairs in major cities like New York or Washington, DC, if you're nearby. I secured at least two internships through career fairs at Howard University. They are a great opportunity to meet with internship coordinators on the spot, which means your interview may be instant. In one case, I was offered an internship on the spot.

Personally, I've completed a handful of internships in college, from paid to unpaid, from TV to radio. I've interned with Showtime Networks' Smithsonian Channel, Fox5 DC, CNN, Blis.FM, and WTOP 103.5 FM. I've also completed fellowships with the Meredith Cronkite program in Arizona and the CBC-UNC Diversity Fellowship in Raleigh, North Carolina. In addition, I've participated in professional development programs through NABJ, such as the Short Courses that are offered to college students majoring in journalism. My paid internships through Showtime Networks and CNN were funded with help from the T. Howard

Foundation. I highly recommend that program to anyone looking for more than an internship. The program is designed to challenge you on how to think deeper about your role as an intern within a company.

- **What to do before you apply for an internship**

The most important thing, before you apply for an internship, is to prepare your resume and cover letter in a professional manner. Most colleges have a career advisor or office where students can get feedback on their resumes and cover letters. Check for spelling and grammatical errors that may disqualify you quickly. Internship coordinators are looking for effort on the part of the applicant. Your past experiences don't have to exactly align with the department you're interning in, but you should try to tailor it as much as possible.

CHAPTER 3

Getting Into Broadcast Journalism, Without a
Broadcast Journalism Degree

Journalism is a field that requires continuous learning on the job. If you didn't go to journalism school and you're interested in journalism, that's okay! Not all journalists were journalism majors starting out. There are all sorts of beats (topics) to cover in journalism, and if you majored in education, science, or psychology, there's a job for you! The key is to be a good writer, an efficient communicator, and possess good ethics.

- **Which journalism school should you attend?**

  "The best journalism school in America is ... a mystery. There's no sensible system for comparing programs or knowing if they are really healthy," according to a 2014 article published by the Knight Foundation.

"A few metrics make sense. Penn State (3,118 students) is the largest; Missouri (1908), the oldest; Columbia, home of the Pulitzer Prize, the most prestigious. North Carolina has won more "overall" Hearst collegiate journalism awards than any other school in the past 15 years; students from Arizona State, the most first place Hearst broadcast awards during that time period; Northwestern, the most writing awards, Western Kentucky, the most photography and multimedia awards." - Knight Foundation

Based on my interactions with the best of the best in the business, the schools mentioned above seem to be some of the most popular. However, if I'm going to be honest, if you really want something, you'll get it done—regardless of where you pursued your degree. I attended Howard University, which is also known for producing some of the best journalists in the country. Still, if I'm being honest, I don't consider it to be 100% the ingredient to my success in journalism.

A lot of factors contributed to the outcome I'm experiencing. Yes, of course, being in the nation's capital has been a dream, and it positioned me to see and do things to which most journalism students didn't have access. However, there were also the fellowships I completed, which exposed me to "the competition." I saw what other journalism schools were like through visits to Arizona State University, Florida Agricultural and Mechanical University (FAMU), and North Carolina A&T State University. All great programs by the way. Although the programs were different, they were similar in many ways. They all have one focus: to produce journalists who have integrity. It's the one thing money can't buy.

The best program for you will hopefully be one that allows you to be as hands-on as possible. The key in journalism is to practice, practice, practice and practice some more. Make the small mistakes early on, so you can tackle the bigger issues later.

Grad School or No Grad School?

If you're like me, and you loved your college experience, you thought about going to grad school right after undergrad. If you're also like me, you're wondering how you'll pay for it. I say go to grad school, if you have the money for it. If you don't, get to work. Journalism jobs don't require a master's degree. They require *experience*. As soon as you can prove that you have some, the higher you'll go.

"At the end of the day, it's an individual and personal choice. Some people learn best in the classroom; others learn well by doing the work," said Muck Rack's Jessica Lawlor.

There are some things that you simply cannot learn in school. The best lessons are learned through repetition and with newsrooms constantly changing, the best lesson plans are available on the job.

CHAPTER 4

*Searching For Your First Job in Broadcast
Journalism*

Once you've decided that you're crazy enough to continue on in the broadcast journalism industry and you've secured a bachelor's degree, now it's time for the hard part. Journalism jobs can be tough to find (especially on-air). Don't panic like I did most of my senior year. Instead, focus on tapping into the networks you've built.

In the meantime, do the groundwork yourself. Start signing up for sites like LinkedIn, TVJobs.com, and Indeed. Once you find the job you're interested in, start working backwards. Check LinkedIn to see if you have a mutual connection (someone you know in real life), so that you can schedule a time to talk to them. During that conversation with them, ask questions about the company and mention that you're applying for a position with their company. In many cases, companies offer a referral credit to employees who refer candidates to positions within their company. It's an incentive for the employee to recommend you and it's an opportunity for your name to be added to the top of the applicant pool.

- **How many rejection e-mails should I expect?**

In an ideal world, you would find a job two days after applying, but in many cases, finding your first job could take months or years, depending on your resume and connections. Whatever the case, pack your patience and trust the process. TV news jobs generally tend to hire quickly, within a month or two. It's best to start applying two to three months from your graduation date, or contract end date.

- **How I landed my first TV news job**

Again, I started working in my first TV news job a week before graduation. It was a quick turnaround between the moment I applied and the moment I accepted the job. I was eager to get my feet wet and it felt like the right decision. A mentor once told me that the best way to navigate the industry is to start in a small market and work your way up. Markets are based on population sizes. The bigger the city, the higher the market.

Before applying to my first job, I was in the middle of a fellowship with WRAL-TV, known as the CBC-UNC Diversity Fellowship. That gave me the opportunity to get some quality clips for my reel and the chance to network with some of the best producers and news managers in the industry. At the time, I was a senior and looking around for jobs.

One of the mentors in the program suggested that I should inform him when I applied for a new job. The moment I applied for WHSV-TV, I told him and he asked around to find me contacts who knew the news director. Through that connection and through his effort, I got a call back and an interview, and the rest was in God's hands. I'm grateful for the divine connection. It was at the right time and under the right circumstances.

Other factors that played a part:
- I also had a resume tape ready four to five months before graduation.
- I have completed at least five internships/fellowships.
- I had mentors who gave me great advice.
- I studied other people's career paths.

The key to finding your first job in journalism is to identify the roles you're passionate about and then focus on the skills you need to acquire in order to meet the qualifications for the job. Which is why internships are so important. Internships are key to identifying the tasks you enjoy and the tasks you dislike.

It's also important to use those internships, as an opportunity to expand your network. The media world is small, so your supervisors may someday become your colleagues. Try to remember as many names as possible. I've seen people land jobs right after an internship, due to excellent networking skills.

CHAPTER 5

Preparing For Your First Job in
Broadcast Journalism

You should prepare for your next step in journalism by considering what it will mean to be a public figure.

Preparation should include:

- Maintaining social media profiles, as if you're already a public figure.

- Preparing financially for a low salary in the beginning, if you plan to try the local news route.

- Getting experience (through internships or jobs).

- Creating a portfolio, including a reel (video montage) and writing samples.

- Working on your resume.

Is a college degree necessary?

In some cases it may not be, but many jobs list it as a requirement. To be on the safe side, I would recommend getting a bachelor's degree.

Can I get a job in a month?

For some people, it can take years to land a job. For others, it may take weeks or months. It depends on the job market, the type of position you're looking for, and how well you're prepared for the role. Landing a producer/reporter position may be easier than landing a job as a news anchor.

It will also be harder for you to land a job if you have nothing to show in your portfolio or on your resume. One of the biggest mistakes I see is a bad resume. Your resume is your first introduction to a potential employer. If there are grammatical errors or misspellings, it's a clear sign you didn't take the time to double-check your work. It's a red flag.

If you're worried your resume isn't up to par, share it with an expert who can review it. A good place to start is at a journalism conference (e.g., NABJ, NAHJ, ONA, IRA, NAB).

Attend a Journalism Conference

Speaking of journalism conferences, you'll want to attend one during your junior or senior year. Why? Because you'll likely meet some of your future peers (also chasing the same goals). You can get advice from them and potentially find a mentor.

It's also a great way to gauge future expectations. At NABJ's conference during my junior year, I had the chance to sit with recruiters, have my reel critiqued, and more. I also met lifelong friends.

Conferences are planned months in advance, so you'll have time to prepare. The most important thing is to think of a strategy for the conference. It's not a vacation or a reason to just hang out. It's a networking opportunity. Here are a few tips on how to successfully navigate a conference.

<u>Dos:</u>

1. Dress professionally
2. Bring business cards and resumes
3. Prepare a resume reel (if interested in on-air jobs)
4. Take notes at workshops
5. After meeting someone at a conference, follow-up with a note to say "thank you."

<u>Don'ts</u>

1. Dress unprofessionally
2. Go unprepared

3. Develop a bad reputation
4. Have a bad attitude
5. Overshare personal information

CHAPTER 6

What Are the Different Types of Jobs in Front of the Camera and Behind the Scenes?

There are lots of jobs that many aren't exposed to in broadcast news, which can be just as rewarding. Pay ranges will vary for each.

- News Director

TV news directors make anywhere from "**$27,370 to $187,200**, with a median salary of $65,530," according to Salary.com in December 2021. Salaries in TV news will vary, based on market sizes. News directors typically hire talent (including reporters, anchors, producers, assignment desk, and web staff). They're heavily involved in conversations with people in charge of the company's brand and the station's finances. You'll hear them discuss things like ratings (which are used to measure the success of the station's newscasts).

Nielsen TV ratings are typically used to measure most stations.

- Assistant News Director

Assistant news directors typically make anywhere from "**$79,849 and $94,364,**" according to Salary.com. The Assistant News Director is typically the new director's right-hand man, filling gaps the news director may have missed. They also work with producers and directors to make sure all shows are clean on-air (aka, flawless).

- General Manager

General Managers are usually rarely seen in the newsroom. They are responsible for ensuring that the company's financial position is on track. That means getting involved with the sales team and the accounting department.

"Among 2,650 general and operations managers in the television broadcasting industry in 2010, the average salary was $135,840 per year," according to CareerTrends.com. "Most employers require a bachelor's degree and at least 10 years of experience in television management. Along with education and experience, successful candidates have experience in sales and operations of a television station, and are knowledgeable of Federal Communications Commission regulations."

Other roles:

- Technical Director
- Production Assistants
- Web producers
- Assignment desk managers/staff
- Associate Producers
- Photojournalists
- Editors

CHAPTER 7

When Is the Right Time to Hire An Agent, If You're An On-Air Talent?

I hired an agent in my third job, because I knew how difficult it would be to move to a bigger market without one. To test that theory, I applied for the same position without an agent and I didn't get the job. The minute my agent helped out, the phones started ringing. Agents make great connections, and they can get you places you never thought possible.

I stumbled into the relationship with my first and only agent, so far. He was recommended by a fellow broadcast journalist. I was a little on the fence about getting an agent in the first place, because you often hear horror stories about agents in the broadcast world. Your relationship with your agent can be a great experience or a bad one. The most important thing is to find an agent who can secure a job on your behalf. I've heard of people paying agents, who aren't able to find them another job, but they were stuck paying said agent. It's a tough situation to be in.

- **How do you choose an agent?**

Most agents have worked with multiple people in the industry. Before signing on the dotted line, you may want to ask around about the agent you're considering. Keep in mind that different people have different experiences with their agents. Not every word should be taken literally. Use the same judgement you would, while sifting through Amazon reviews.

I would not recommend getting an agent in your first job, perhaps your second or third. In your first job, you may not make enough to pay all your bills, much less an agent. In your second job, things may improve, but perhaps not dramatically. In other words, wait until you can afford an agent.

The rates for TV agents aren't all the same.

"It can vary. The average is between 4 and 5% (some pay 7%, others pay 1%). The numbers vary depending on such things as your salary, how long you've been with us, how long you've been at a particular station, etc.," said TV news talent agency DCA TV, in a response to frequently asked questions.

CHAPTER 8

The Pros and Cons of Social Media

I'm a little excited to share details about my personal experience with social media and the pros and cons. If you've followed me for a while, you know my views on social media. It's a tool for reaching my audience and I've read books on how to use social media in a productive way. It's a great tool for connecting with people in the community and for finding story ideas. I found lots of stories through social media in the DMV. As a verified user on Twitter, you can use it to your advantage to reach potential interview subjects.

Most recently, I had an experience where a social media post was used without my permission. I felt violated. I won't get into it too much, due to privacy reasons. Hashtag IYKYK.

Lessons from incident:

Interactions don't tell the true story about your social media following. Sometimes there are more people checking on your posts than you may think. You may only have 400 to 500 likes on a post, but you may have 5,000 eyeballs on that post. Strange right? Why does that matter? Basically, you just never know who's watching. Try to avoid anything that may be misinterpreted (e.g., t-shirts, inside jokes, etc.).

Privacy is a premium on social media. I'm at a stage where I prefer to share career updates and news through social media, without giving away too much about my social or personal life. In the age of TikTok, you should still think of your social media profile as a professional website. Remember, you never know who is watching. Even though you may have a false sense of privacy due to limited interactions. Also, you never know how long your videos may remain accessible on the Internet after being reshared thousands of times.

"White male reporters are given the benefit of the doubt more often," said Maria Polletta, an investigative reporter for the Arizona Center for Investigative Reporting. "If you're a person of color, a woman, a member of any kind of minority group, there's automatically judgments made based on how objective or fair you can be."

Polletta spoke to the Columbia Journalism Review for an article entitled "A Twitter tightrope without a net: Journalists' reactions to newsroom social media policies." The piece written by Jacob Nelson was published in December 2021, "it draws on interviews with 37 reporters, editors, publishers, freelancers, and social media/audience engagement managers from throughout the U.S. about their experiences with and thoughts about their newsrooms' social media policies." I would highly recommend checking it out.

"The inconsistent enforcement of these policies leaves women journalists and journalists of color feeling doubly disadvantaged: They are insufficiently protected from the abuse they are more likely to receive, and unfairly singled out for using social media," Nelson said.

Social media can be a dangerous place, in general. Use it strategically and be mindful of the things you share.

CHAPTER 9

The State of the Media Industry

On October 27, 2021, I woke up to a trending article from an industry blog. The Cronkite News Lab published an article entitled "The Local Newsroom Recruitment Crisis (Part 1)." The article took a deeper look at the factors leading to "The Great Resignation," as it has been coined.

Some of the factors mentioned:

- **Lack of competitive salaries**

Multimedia journalists, also known as MMJs or one-man bands, are still making roughly $30,000 in their first jobs. For many, who do have student loans, that's unacceptable and hard to commit to for more than a year.

"I cannot tell you how often I am hearing from news directors who know that working at a restaurant, or at a fast-food place, or doing some manufacturing job, those jobs are paying extraordinarily more money. We're talking about 30 to 40% more," a newsroom coach told Cronkite's Andrew Heyward in December 2021.

- **Options**

With more companies offering media-related jobs to keep up with the growing social media market, young journalists now have more options. Some of my former colleagues have left the business to pursue similar careers with large tech companies.

"You can struggle for $30,000 and have three roommates and maybe get food stamps, or you can earn a good living almost anywhere in the country, working in corporate communications," Syracuse Newhouse adjunct professor Bob Papper said. "Graduates of journalism programs are finding compelling alternatives to the newsroom, not just in PR and marketing but at companies increasingly interested in creating original content."

- **Larger markets recruiting college students**

Networks are also hiring more college students for entry-level jobs, making it harder for smaller markets to retain talent and creating more competition.

I urge you all to take the time to read Sydney Cameron's blog post entitled "Why I left TV News." It's available on her site SydneyCameron.com.

"The TV news industry is a 24/7 beast with a stone-cold heart. You become a slave to it, planning your life around ratings months (February, May, July, & November) when most stations institute vacation black-out dates," she said. *"I planned my wedding around it, my sister planned her wedding around it, and my two pregnancies and children's birth dates were meticulously thought out because I wanted to be able to take time off to celebrate when those special dates rolled around."*

I share all of this not to discourage you from pursuing your dreams of one day being in this business, but to encourage you to think about all the pros and cons that may not be readily available to you. It's something I wish I did more of, before embarking on this journey.

CHAPTER 10

Does Market Size Matter?

I get this question a lot. The answer isn't black and white. My short answer: it depends. It depends on your values. If you value a big city life, with possibly more money, you may enjoy a larger market. Again, market sizes are based on population sizes.

These days, it's possible to start your first job in TV in whichever market you'd like, but the question is: should you? The best advice I've ever received is to start small and make your mistakes in places where no one can see those mistakes, especially if you're an on-air reporter juggling multiple roles for the first time. Imagine starting in a large market like DC or New York and then getting fired for constantly making small mistakes. It's a marathon, not a sprint. Take time to develop the skills needed to perform for when you get to the next stage.

My question to you is, "What are your values?" For me, getting back to DC wasn't a result of the market size, but mainly because I love the area. It's the closest thing I've ever gotten to feeling at home, besides being in Jamaica. It was more about that feeling, but the market size was a plus.

My biggest advice is to find a city that makes you feel whole. You can spend your life working, but never feel whole. Having family and friends nearby makes all the difference when it comes to your comfort level, and it also reflects in your work. People can tell when you're happy to be in their city.

If you're someone with a family, who wants to avoid the hustle and bustle of big cities and the high cost of living, you may enjoy a smaller city. So, it really depends on where you are in life. I will say bigger markets tend to have more resources, in terms of manpower, money, and more. In my first market (#178 at the time), I didn't have a photographer. In DC and Louisville, I did. Also, larger markets are often feeders for large networks like CNN or their affiliates, which could also be a good stepping-stone if you're interested in moving on to a network.

- **Perks of moving to a larger market**

  Larger markets do tend to offer more money, but the thing to pay attention to is the ratio between the salary and the cost of living in the city you're going to. If you're living in New York City, making $100,000 may not be as much as you think. The cost of rent and food will far outweigh the salary.

CHAPTER 11

Safety Tips for MMJs

By now, many of you have seen a horrific video shared on social media of reporter Tori Yorgey being hit by a car on-air in January 2022. The video sent shockwaves in the journalism community, and especially among the MMJ community. It proved what we all know to be true. Multi-media journalists, also known as one-man bands, have a tough job.

The video of Yorgey's solo live-shot mishap garnered so much attention that some journalists even started a petition against one-man band live shots. Some have claimed that solo live shots are dangerous in more ways than one. In the group known as Becoming Storytellers (on Instagram), some shared their firsthand experiences on January 25, 2022. "I once had to knock on a pedophile's door for an interview on the charges as an MMJ in my first market. Totally alone.

No thought given from management on how bad that was," one person wrote. Another person wrote, "I was sent alone to a shooting ("breaking news" the day after) where there was obviously no longer going to be a police presence, and a man threatened to rape me and said he would use my camera 'to make porno out of it.'"

The stories are horrifying and real. One of the questions to ask your future employer, before accepting a job, is, "Will I be required to run my own live shots?" If the answer is yes, then you should consider turning down the job—unless the hiring manager promises that the live shots will only be necessary in situations that are not dangerous.

My Personal Experience With 'MMJing'

I did not have many horror stories with live shots starting out, minus the extreme nervousness I felt. Thankfully, my news director at the time did not believe in solo live shots. She never explained why, but I'm now thankful she made that decision.

To be honest, I only did it for ten months. That was all I could withstand. It was mentally and emotionally draining. You're doing multiple jobs in one, including acting as a videographer, producer, reporter, web editor, fashion stylist, makeup artist and sometimes even a producer. Cutting corners on so many positions can lead to many errors, which is why many smaller markets are known for MMJs and known for being "places where you can make mistakes."

I tried to keep safety top of mind when doing live shots as an MMJ. Doing live shots, in general, requires a lot of attention to your surroundings. Sometimes people shout obscenities in the middle of your live shots. They may approach you while under the influence. They may even sneak up behind you and touch you. We've seen it all at this point.

Safety Tips

- **Try to avoid sharing your exact location**

In my first job, one thing my company stressed was to avoid sharing your location, via social media, during a live shot. The warning came after a young reporter was killed during a live shot by a "disgruntled former colleague" in 2015.

I understand that this may not always be possible to accomplish, but it's worth thinking about your environment before posting. Do you feel safe? Are you surrounded by officers or security, while covering a story late at night or early in the morning? How long will you be in the area? Will you stay in the same spot? Will it be easy to find you, based on the photo? I know it may seem a little obsessive, but always keep safety first.

Messages on Social Media

Some people develop stalkers. The best way to try to avoid that is to limit how much personal information you're sharing. Easier said than done, when you're told to open up, so people can get to know you, to increase your popularity on social media. However, when it comes to things like messages from strangers, unless it's directly related to a story you're working on, you should probably avoid them, especially when the messages are focused on your physical appearance. Keep it professional with viewers to avoid any conflicts of interest and obsessive behavior.

CHAPTER 12

Job Searching Tips

L ooking for a new job can be challenging for sure, in the moment you're anxious and eager to land a new position. It's always best to slow down your thoughts and really examine the qualities you're looking for in a company. For me, as I get older, that now includes work-life balance, competitive benefits, a decent vacation policy, maternity leave, and more.

- **Hours**

The hours are also an important factor, especially in newsrooms. If you're not a morning person, do *not* sign up for a morning shift. If you're not a night person, do *not* sign up for a nightside shift. You see where I'm going with this?

Working holidays is an inevitable part of journalism. We're always *on*. If that's a deal breaker for you, you should reconsider the career path you're heading down.

- **Values**

It also includes ensuring that the company's values match your values. Research the owners of the company, headlines about the company's reputation, and recent lawsuits filed against the company. It's easier said than done, when you're just trying to get your foot in the door at a company, but it will be worth it.

Also, read the company's mission statement on their website. Do you like what you see? Does it reflect who you are? Are there hidden messages that you don't agree with?

- **Doing your research about the position you're applying for**

Let's say you get to the part where you get invited for an interview and the hiring managers are excited about giving you an offer. You may want to start looking around at the people inside the newsroom. How long have they been there? What's the turnover rate like? Who was in your position before they started searching for someone to fill the position? These are all questions you should be asking yourself.

- **Reaching out to other employees for background information**

Reaching out to current employees at a company you're interested in can be a tricky situation. Most current employees don't want to share everything about the state of their company for several reasons. It may be wise to find a future colleague who knows a mutual friend. It's a small industry. You'd be surprised by who knows who.

If you do reach out to someone on your own, be respectful. Remember that they are not obligated to share information with you. You can ask questions like: How do you like your current position? What are the pros and cons there? Who was in my position last? What's the workflow like? Are there growth opportunities? What are the perks of the contracts?

Contracts

Lastly, let's talk about contracts. Those legally binding documents can be very intimidating. You may have an agent who is not an attorney who can't break them down into layman's terms, or you may be negotiating your contracts on your own. Just remember, not all contracts are created equal.

Some contracts are better than others, and some contracts are more restrictive than others. It's okay to go back to the drawing board and request changes, where needed. One of the things that people forget to ask for in broadcast journalism contracts are "outs." Outs can allow you to make a market jump, while in the middle of a contract. For example, you can have an "out" for a top 50 market, after a year at a station, allowing you to leave a station more quickly if you so choose.

You could also ask for a shorter contract upfront, before you sign a contract. You may be offered a three-year contract at your first job, but you don't have to accept that original offer. You could request a shorter contract, which may be countered with a slightly lower salary.

If you're an on-air talent, you should also request a clothing or makeup stipend, because appearances are a huge part of the job. I had a makeup stipend in my first market and it really helped. Some stations even cover the cost of dry cleaning your clothes, especially when you're an anchor. In general, find out what perks can be added to the contract.

CHAPTER 13

Mistakes to Avoid

I would be lying if I told you I was perfect. I'm not perfect. I've made mistakes in my career. One of them being social media. Social media can be a powerful tool for connecting with viewers and like-minded people, but it can also be a place where people hide behind keyboards.

Be careful about what you post. If a post can be misinterpreted, think twice about posting it. Some people have a professional and a personal account for this reason. There are sites that will gossip on blogs about your social media choices, because it's profitable for them. Some of the most popular issues that the sites gossip about are TV personalities' appearances, their tweets, the locations where they take their selfies (e.g., at a crime scene), and anything to do with politics.

In an industry this small, you may also want to be careful about who you share certain information with, because it may somehow end up on one of those sites. It's important to gatekeep information about your personal and professional life. Try to keep those two worlds as separate as possible.

I hope you enjoyed this book. There are no hard and fast rules in this industry, but I hope this gives you a better understanding of things to do when you're starting out. There is no magic roadmap in journalism. It's an industry that you'll have to figure out as you progress. You never know when a new opportunity may come knocking at the door, as companies create new positions to fill gaps caused by innovation.

www.ingramcontent.com/pod-product-compliance
Lightning Source LLC
Chambersburg PA
CBHW020343130626
46549CB00003B/1262